SUPER SENTENCES

SUPER SENTENCES

A VOCABULARY BUILDING ACTIVITY BOOK FOR WORD LOVERS
OF ALL AGES, INCLUDING SCHOOL AGE CHILDREN.

SUSAN WINEBRENNER, M.S.

authorHOUSE®

AuthorHouse™ LLC
1663 Liberty Drive
Bloomington, IN 47403
www.authorhouse.com
Phone: 1-800-839-8640

Published by AuthorHouse   09/09/2013

ISBN: 978-1-4817-7213-6 (sc)
ISBN: 978-1-4817-7212-9 (e)

Library of Congress Control Number: 2013912161

AN INTRODUCTION TO SUPER SENTENCES

This book contains twenty-two SUPER SENTENCES at two levels of difficulty. The chart on this page gives a rough idea of the appropriate grades for each level.

These sentences have been successfully used in classroom situations to provide a challenging activity in vocabulary that includes all levels of Bloom's Taxonomy. Students must know how to use the dictionary, thesaurus, and pronunciation keys; comprehend the syntax of words and the parts of speech; be able to apply skills learned in reading, English and language arts in the SUPER SENTENCE setting; analyze the most sensible way to put the words together for coherent meaning, and evaluate how well they are creating meaningful thoughts throughout the activity.

Since this activity is so challenging, students should be able to work together in pairs or triads so they may constantly check out the sense of their work with each other.

	Above Average Ability	*Average Ability*	*Below Average Ability*
Level One	Grades 3 & 4	Grades 5 & 6	Grades 7-12
Level Two	Grades 5-12	Grades 7-12	

Materials

Each student should have a copy of the selected SUPER SENTNCE, as well as a hard copy or online version, of an advanced level dictionary. For Level Two sentences, the dictionary must be unabridged.

Directions for Use

1. The teacher distributes one copy to each student working on the same sentence and reads the sentences aloud several times. From the inflections and points of emphasis in the teacher's voice, the students are to determine the part of speech of each capitalized word. The teacher makes sure all students have the correct part of speech identified. They write the abbreviation for the parts of speech above each word and use this information to select the correct entry in the dictionary.

2. The teacher guides the students to discover the root words in each capitalized word to simplify the work in the dictionary. Students draw a box or circle around the root words.

3. Students work to complete the chart below each sentence. At least one or two days of class time are recommended. In addition, the students should have several days to work independently, practicing with each other for correct pronunciation and translation.

Students may write out their versions of the translation in the space provided at the bottom of each page, or on the back of the paper.

4. The group meets again with the teacher to demonstrate they have learned the words. Moving around a circle formation, each student reads only that part of each sentence up to and including a capitalized word. The recitation continues through several cycles, which gives students the opportunity to pronounce a different word each time. At some point, some student will ask to try to read the sentence in its entirety. Give several students a chance to do this, and then perhaps the whole group can read the sentence in unison. Up to this point, no definitions are included.

5. Using the same technique as in step 4, students take turns sharing their definitions for each word. Differences of interpretation are discussed and students may make appropriate changes in their own work for accuracy.

6. Students now take turns translating the entire sentence. Some may wish to recite it from memory at this point.

7. If grading is required, which is **not recommended**, each member of a pair or triad should get the same grade. The grade should reflect the effort in completing the chart, as well as the students' success in translation. Do not correct or grade the content of the chart. Students should only be evaluated on how well they can use that information to pronounce and translate the sentence. Do not test the students on the words out of context as this will surely extinguish their enthusiasm for the activity.

Extension Activity

Some students may wish to create their own sentences, alone or as part of a team. This is an excellent way to teach use of the thesaurus.

A natural follow-up is for students to "transmogrify" familiar phrases or stories from simple to complex and/or surprising. This works best if students first write out a one or two page summary of a well-known story, folk, or fairy tale, and then transmogrify the summary. In this activity, students usually prefer to work alone and are encouraged to keep the actual title of their story a secret from others. Students may also work together at the teacher's discretion, But all students are required to participate in the circle activity described in #4 above INDEPENDENTLY. The teacher reads the completed transmogrification aloud to the entire class until several students can guess the original story. Other sources for transmogrifications include proverbs and pithy sayings. Activities in the study of etymology, the history of words, are also related and appropriate.

CAUTION: The completed sheet is used for the students as they translate the sentence, and evaluation should be confined to the students' ability to provide a sensible translation. It is fine to leave lots of room for interpretation on the chart, as long as the student's translation makes sense.

This activity will provide much enjoyment for your students, and even for their friends and families. Enjoy watching your students get turned on to the excitement of the English language and to the history of words. Students should be encouraged to create their own Super Sentences, even with help from their families! Great examples can be made available for other students to enjoy. Of course, answer keys must accompany any student/family submitted Super Sentence. Students should also be supported in their efforts to use some of the words they learn in their own writing.

Feel free to submit some of these sentences to Susan through her website, www.susanwinebrenner.com. Who knows, they might even appear in a future version of the e-book edition of Super Sentences, so be sure to include contact information for the submitting student so the author can reach them to secure their permission. Students may also submit their claims that some words in this book are mis-spelled or mis-defined. Susan will return their queries post-haste!

Above all, everyone involved should have lots of fun!

PRONUNCIATION KEY

ə	as in banana, level	ow	as in pout, fowl
a	as in pad, fat	sh	as in shout, shy
ā	as in made, vacation	th	as in thread, thick
ä	as in all, saw	<u>th</u>	as in this, neither
ch	as in check	u	as in fun, hum
e	as in bed, met	ü	as in school, rule
ē	as in meat, free	u̇	as in foot, put
i	as in did, lip	âr	as in far
ī	as in died, mine	ār	as in air, dare
j	as in juice, just, gentle	êr	as in perk
k	as in cookie, kitchen	ēr	as in ear, weird
ng	as in finger, sing	îr	as in sir
o	as in hot, pod	ôr	as in fort
ō	as in home, know	ûr	as in fur
ȯ	as in dot, bother	yu	as in youth, few
oi	as in destroy, boy, noise	y̌u	as in cure, fury
oy	as in boy, joy		
oo	as in ooze, boo	zh	as in vision

Level One

SUPER SENTENCES

We live near a GROTESQUE, HIDEOUS, DETERIORATED old house, filled with TORTUOUS, IMPENETRABLE hallways which give me EERIE, GHASTLY feelings of CLAUSTROPHOBIA and TREPIDATION, especially when I hear the FORMIDABLE CACOPHONY of BABBLING voices when no one is there!

WORD	PRONUNCIATION	MEANING

Level One—Sentence 1 © *Super Sentences* by Susan Winebrenner, Bloomington IN: AuthorHouse, 2013.

"Translation into Everyday Language"

_____

_____

_____

_____

SUPER SENTENCES

An ABSENTMINDED professor, whose summer HABITAT was a DISMAL SHANTY, was FLABBERGASTED to learn he had been DULY BEQUEATHED a FASHIONABLE, PALATIAL MANSION in a LUXURIOUS, GENTEEL neighborhood.

WORD	PRONUNCIATION	MEANING

Level One—Sentence 2 © *Super Sentences* by Susan Winebrenner, Bloomington IN: AuthorHouse, 2013.

"Translation into Everyday Language"

_____

_____

_____

_____

_____

SUPER SENTENCES

"Automan," the MECHANICAL, AMBIDEXTROUS robot we own to do our MENIAL chores, caused a FRENETIC HULLABALOO when his CIRCUITS became INOPERABLE, and he ran AMOK CAPRICIOUSLY through our house, DEFACING everything in his path and leaving IMPASSABLE PANDEMONIUM everywhere.

WORD	PRONUNCIATION	MEANING

Level One—Sentence 3 © Super Sentences by Susan Winebrenner, Bloomington IN: AuthorHouse Publishing, 2013.

"Translation into Everyday Language"

_____

_____

_____

_____

_____

SUPER SENTENCES

In the FABULOUS, GRANDIOSE CHATEAU, which has an INCOMPARABLY IMPRESSIVE, PANORAMIC view of the surrounding TERRAIN, the GORGEOUS CHANDELIER swayed OMINOUSLY, seconds before the LETHAL earthquake struck.

WORD	PRONUNCIATION	MEANING

Level One—Sentence 4 © Super Sentences by Susan Winebrenner, Bloomington IN: AuthorHouse Publishing, 2013.

"Translation into Everyday Language"

_____

_____

_____

_____

_____

SUPER SENTENCES

My parents AGONIZED over whether to buy me a computer game with which I was ENAMORED, or a radio-controlled airplane, which I LOATHED. My BERSERK behavior let them know I was DEVASTATED by their choice, and they let me know they RESENTED my OBJECTIONABLE, REBELLIOUS, TEMPERAMENTAL reaction, and ADMONISHED me EARNESTLY to remember that everyone is FALLIBLE.

WORD	PRONUNCIATION	MEANING

Level One—Sentence 5 © Super Sentences by Susan Winebrenner, Bloomington IN: AuthorHouse Publishing, 2013.

"Translation into Everyday Language"

_____

_____

_____

_____

SUPER SENTENCES

My uncle, an GOURMAND, with his usual APLOMB, approached the table at my cousin's wedding BANQUET with such ALACRITY (OBVIOUSLY lacking ADEQUATE FORESIGHT) that he INGESTED what he thought was a PALATABLE DELICACY, which was actually the table's centerpiece. How GAUCHE!

WORD	PRONUNCIATION	MEANING

Level One—Sentence 6 © Super Sentences by Susan Winebrenner, Bloomington IN: AuthorHouse Publishing, 2013.

"Translation into Everyday Language"

_____

_____

_____

_____

_____

SUPER SENTENCES

At the circus, a FOOLHARDY, LOQUACIOUS HAWKER stood in a GARGANTUAN, GARISHLY decorated wagon, trying to BAMBOOZLE and BEFUDDLE the people in the crowd, using LINGO to sell them a CONCOCTION which he ASSERTED would allow kids to PROCURE all A's in school if they IMBIBED one teaspoonful every morning.

WORD	PRONUNCIATION	MEANING

Level One—Sentence 7 © Super Sentences by Susan Winebrenner, Bloomington IN: AuthorHouse Publishing, 2013.

"Translation into Everyday Language"

_____

_____

_____

_____

_____

SUPER SENTENCES

Because she had DETECTED CHRONIC DEFICIENCIES in our spelling recently, our teacher declared an ULTIMATUM: either we RECTIFY the DECLINE in our scores and ACCRUE several CONSECUTIVE TRIUMPHS, or we would have to FORFEIT our place as the FOREMOST CONTRIBUTORS to the school newspaper.

WORD	PRONUNCIATION	MEANING

Level One—Sentence 8 © Super Sentences by Susan Winebrenner, Bloomington IN: AuthorHouse Publishing, 2013.

"Translation into Everyday Language"

_____

_____

_____

_____

_____

SUPER SENTENCES

At the FESTIVE, TESTIMONIAL REPAST for our FLAMBOYANT, DAPPER, DEBONAIR principal, the guests ate RAVENOUSLY all the DELECTABLE TIDBITS which had been PAINSTAKINGLY prepared by our P.T.A.'s ENTERPRISING experts in the CULINARY arts.

WORD	PRONUNCIATION	MEANING

Level One—Sentence 9 © Super Sentences by Susan Winebrenner, Bloomington IN: AuthorHouse Publishing, 2013.

"Translation into Everyday Language"

_____

_____

_____

SUPER SENTENCES

Tigers can be SAVAGE, FEROCIOUS, COMBATIVE animals. Tiger trainers should not be too ARROGANT or CONCEITED, or they might have to GRAPPLE DEFENSIVELY with a VORACIOUS, BELLIGERENT CARNIVORE that would UNEQUIVOCALLY be VICTORIOUS.

WORD	PRONUNCIATION	MEANING

Level One—Sentence 10 © Super Sentences by Susan Winebrenner, Bloomington IN: AuthorHouse Publishing, 2013.

"Translation into Everyday Language"

_____

_____

_____

_____

_____

SUPER SENTENCES

For a career in AERONAUTICS, PREREQUISITES include: a DAUNTLESS, HEROIC spirit, no QUEASINESS or ACROPHOBIA, the ability to SKILLFULLY operate TECHNICAL APPARATUS, and an ENERGETIC DEVOTION to the GLORY of American dominance in space.

WORD	PRONUNCIATION	MEANING

Level One—Sentence 11 © Super Sentences by Susan Winebrenner, Bloomington IN: AuthorHouse Publishing, 2013.

"Translation into Everyday Language"

_____

_____

_____

_____

_____

Level Two

SUPER SENTENCES

The CAITIFF USURPER, ACCOUTERED for MARAUDING with his JUNTA, sought IMPERIUM for the MOBOCRACY, unaware of the ANIMUS of the IMPUISSANT, LUMPEN DEMURRERS ready to IMMOLATE themselves for the sake of their cause.

WORD	PRONUNCIATION	MEANING

Level Two—Sentence 1 © Super Sentences by Susan Winebrenner, Bloomington IN: AuthorHouse Publishing, 2013.

"Translation into Everyday Language"

_____

_____

_____

_____

_____

SUPER SENTENCES

The PRODIGIOUS and PROLIFIC COGNOSCENTE of modern music, FESTINATING to TRANSCRIBE the SCHERZO for winds and TIMPANI, TRUNCATED it to make a SEGUE between the ITERATIVE, ANTIPHONAL, and ISACOUSTIC sections of his new composition.

WORD	PRONUNCIATION	MEANING

Level Two—Sentence 2 © Super Sentences by Susan Winebrenner, Bloomington IN: AuthorHouse Publishing, 2013.

"Translation into Everyday Language"

_____

_____

_____

_____

_____

SUPER SENTENCES

The BRAGGADOCIO of the POETASTER is apparent as he writes his CLOYING DITHYRAMBS for ACCOLADES alone; while the ORGULOUS IAMBOGRAPHER has the METTLE and PANACHE to EXCOGITATE his LAMPOONS without GASCONADE.

WORD	PRONUNCIATION	MEANING

Level Two—Sentence 3 © Super Sentences by Susan Winebrenner, Bloomington IN: AuthorHouse Publishing, 2013.

"Translation into Everyday Language"

_____

_____

_____

_____

_____

SUPER SENTENCES

The SENESCENT MYSTAGOGUE, DIVAGATING from LUCULENT interpretations and SPOUTING ABSTRUSE CANT, MESMERIZED the PURBLIND NEOPHYTES who were AGOG at his supposed SAGACITY.

WORD	PRONUNCIATION	MEANING

Level Two—Sentence 4 © Super Sentences by Susan Winebrenner, Bloomington IN: AuthorHouse Publishing, 2013.

"Translation into Everyday Language"

_____

_____

_____

_____

_____

SUPER SENTENCES

On a CHIVY with our FOWLING PIECES, we approached the CISMONTANE as an UNFORTUITOUS LEVANTER blew down. Encountering a SCREE, a CHAMOIS, and the EFFLUVIUMS of TRAVERTINES, we HOVE our rope, HEEZED ourselves up, and listened to a strange DIAPASON.

WORD	PRONUNCIATION	MEANING

Level Two—Sentence 5 © Super Sentences by Susan Winebrenner, Bloomington IN: AuthorHouse Publishing, 2013.

"Translation into Everyday Language"

_____

_____

_____

_____

SUPER SENTENCES

The visiting PRELATE, INDAGATING MULTIFARIOUS aspects of TRADITIONALISM by virtue of his ACUMEN, labored in the CHANCEL by the SACRISTY door, resisting the impulse to SQUIB a POLEMICAL PAEAN which would have been a CONTRETEMPS to his colleagues in the CALEFACTORY.

WORD	PRONUNCIATION	MEANING

"Translation into Everyday Language"

_____

_____

_____

_____

_____

SUPER SENTENCES

The MEED for the PROFLIGATE GORMANDIZER, whose IRREFRAGABLY CORPULENT PHYSIOGNOMY betrayed his UNABSTEMIOUS HYPOSTASIS, and who refused to hold in ABEYANCE his DRACONIC appetite, was DYSPEPSIA and KATZENJAMMER.

WORD	PRONUNCIATION	MEANING

Level Two—Sentence 7 © Super Sentences by Susan Winebrenner, Bloomington IN: AuthorHouse Publishing, 2013.

"Translation into Everyday Language"

_____

_____

_____

_____

_____

SUPER SENTENCES

The UNCONSCIONABLE MALFEASANTS of the KAKISTOCRACY had a PROCLIVITY to PRATE INDEFATIGABLY in their own ARGOT and would JUGULATE any TIMOROUS PROSELYTE who held an opinion MINACIOUS or PARLOUS to them.

WORD	PRONUNCIATION	MEANING

Level Two—Sentence 8 © Super Sentences by Susan Winebrenner, Bloomington IN: AuthorHouse Publishing, 2013.

"Translation into Everyday Language"

_____

_____

_____

_____

_____

SUPER SENTENCES

In CARTOMANCY, PRESTIDIGITATORS who use OBFUSCATION and PETTIFOGGERY may live in OBLOQUY if a CHARY, INDEFECTIBLE HARBINGER of justice arises whose ONUS is to expose the FEIGNED VERSIMILITUDE of the practitioners as CHICANERY.

WORD	PRONUNCIATION	MEANING

Level Two—Sentence 9 © Super Sentences by Susan Winebrenner, Bloomington IN: AuthorHouse Publishing, 2013.

"Translation into Everyday Language"

_____

_____

_____

_____

SUPER SENTENCES

The MEWLING, INCONTINENT NEONATES are PURPORTED to REEK VENIAL, NOISOME FETORS similar to those EMINATING from a NOXIOUS, MEPHITIC CARAVANSERAI.

WORD	PRONUNCIATION	MEANING

Level Two—Sentence 10 © Super Sentences by Susan Winebrenner, Bloomington IN: AuthorHouse Publishing, 2013.

"Translation into Everyday Language"

_____

_____

_____

_____

_____

SUPER SENTENCES

The TRUCULENT, OPPIDAN LICKSPITTLE SEQUESTERED himself from the BROUHAHA caused by the PUSILLANIMOUS MOUNTEBANK, and MACHINATED a MACHIAVELLIAN PREVARICATION to METE to himself some of the mountebank's LUCRE.

WORD	PRONUNCIATION	MEANING

Level Two—Sentence 11 © Super Sentences by Susan Winebrenner, Bloomington IN: AuthorHouse Publishing, 2013.

"Translation into Everyday Language"

_____

_____

_____

_____

_____

Answer Keys

LEVEL ONE ANSWERS

We live near a GROTESQUE, HIDEOUS, DETERIORATED old house, filled with TORTUOUS, IMPENETRABLE hallways which give me EERIE, GHASTLY feelings of CLAUSTROPHOBIA and TREPIDATION, especially when I hear the FORMIDABLE CACOPHONY of BABBLING voices when no one is there!

Word	*Pronunciation*	*Meaning*
grotesque (adj)	grō tesk'	distorted or absurd in appearance or shape
hideous (adj)	hid' ē əs	very ugly; revolting to look at
deteriorated (adj)	də ter' ē ər ā təd	run down; in need of repair
tortuous (adj)	tôr' choo əs	full of twists and turns
impenetrable (adj)	im pen' ə trə bəl	incapable of being penetrated
eerie (adj)	ē' rē	weird, strange
ghastly (adj)	gast' lē	horrible, frightful
claustrophobia (n)	klos trə tō' bē ə	fear of closed-in places
trepidation (n)	trep ə dā' shun	fear or dread
formidable (adj)	fôr' mi də bəl	awesome, dreadful
cacophony (n)	kə käf' ə ne	mixture of sounds that do not blend
babbling (adj)	bab' ling	foolish, confused talking

TRANSLATION

We live near an absurd-looking, ugly, run-down old house, filled with twisting halls that are impossible to get through, which give me weird, frightened feelings of the fear of being in a closed-in place, especially when I hear the dreadful, horrible-sounding noise of foolishly talking voices when no one is there.

31

SUPER SENTENCE 2	**Level One**

An ABSENTMINDED professor, whose summer HABITAT was a DISMAL SHANTY, was FLABBERGASTED to learn he had been DULY BEQUEATHED a FASHIONABLE, PALATIAL MANSION in a LUXURIOUS GENTEEL neighborhood.

Word	*Pronunciation*	*Meaning*
absentminded (adj)	ab' sent mīn dəd	preoccupied, forgetful
habitat (n)	hab' ə tat	place where one is commonly found, living area
dismal (adj)	diz' məl	dreary, cheerless
shanty (n)	shan' tē	crude building, usually temporary, shack
flabbergasted (v)	flab' bêr gas təd	shocked, overwhelmed
duly (adv)	doo' lē	properly, as is right and fitting
bequeathed (v)	bə kwēthd'	left something in a will
fashionable (adj)	fa' shun ə bəl	stylish
palatial (adj)	pə lā' shəl	like a palace
mansion (n)	man' shun	large home with many rooms
luxurious (adj)	lug shûr' ē əs	rich, very comfortable
genteel (adj)	jen tēl'	upperclass, elegant

TRANSLATION

A forgetful professor who lived in the summer in a cheerless, dreary shack, was shocked to learn he had been fittingly left, as a gift from someone who had died, a stylish, palace-like, huge home in a rich, elegant neighborhood.

| **SUPER SENTENCE 3** | **Level One** |

"Automan," the MECHANICAL, AMBIDEXTROUS robot we own to do our MENIAL chores, caused a FRENETIC HULLABALOO when his CIRCUITS became INOPERABLE, and he ran AMOK CAPRICIOUSLY through our house, DEFACING everything in his path and leaving IMPASSABLE PANDEMONIUM everywhere.

Word	*Pronunciation*	*Meaning*
mechanical (adj)	mə kan' i kəl	operated automatically as by machine
ambidextrous (adj)	am bi dek' strəs	using both hands with equal ease
menial (adj)	mē' nē əl	a job that requires no special skill
frenetic (adj)	frə ne' tik	hurried; disordered; hectic
hullabaloo (n)	həl'ə bə l̄oo	confused noise; uproar
circuits (n)	sîr' kuts	the path traveled by electricity
inoperable (adj)	in op' êr ə bəl	unable to be used
amok (adv)	ə mək'	in a violently excited manner
capriciously (adv)	kə prish' əs lē	likely to change suddenly; impulsively
defacing (v)	də fā' sing	damaging the surface of something
impassable (adj)	im pas' ə bəl	impossible to move through
pandemonium (n)	pan də mō' nē əm	wild disorder

TRANSLATION

"Automan," the automatic robot we own to do our simple chores, who could use his right and left hands with equal ease, caused a disordered uproar when his electrical pathways became impossible to operate, and he ran impulsively, in a violently excited manner, through our house, damaging the surfaces of everything in his path and leaving wild disorder everywhere through which it was impossible to move.

SUPER SENTENCE 4	**Level One**

In the FABULOUS, GRANDIOSE CHATEAU, which has an INCOMPARABLY IMPRESSIVE, PANORAMIC view of the surrounding TERRAIN, the GORGEOUS CHANDELIER swayed OMINOUSLY, seconds before the LETHAL earthquake struck.

Word	Pronunciation	Meaning
fabulous (adj)	fab' yoo ləs	wonderful; incredible
grandiose (adj)	gran dē ōs'	imposing and showy
chateau (n)	sha tō'	a large country house
incomparably (adj)	in kom' pêt ə blē	incapable of being compared
impressive (adj)	im pres' iv	making a mark or impression
panoramic (adj)	pan er am' ik	unlimited view in all directions
terrain (n)	têr rān'	the feature of the land
gorgeous (adj)	gôr' jus	dazzlingly beautiful
chandelier (n)	shan də lēr'	crystal light hanging from the ceiling
commodious (adj)	kə mō' dē əs	unconfining, affording ample space
ominously (adv)	om' in Estate lē	suggesting that danger is coming
lethal (adj)	lē' thəl	causing death

TRANSLATION

In the incredibly wonderful and showy country house, which has an unlimited view of all the land around it that makes such a wonderful impression that it cannot be compared, the beautiful light fixture in the spacious room swayed, telling of coming danger, seconds before a killing earthquake struck.

SUPER SENTENCE 5 | **Level One**

My parents AGONIZED over whether to buy me a computer game with which I was ENAMORED, or a radio-controlled airplane, which I LOATHED. My BERSERK behavior let them know I was DEVASTATED by their choice, and they let me know they RESENTED my OBJECTIONABLE, REBELLIOUS, TEMPERAMENTAL reaction, and ADMONISHED me EARNESTLY to remember that everyone is FALLIBLE.

Word	Pronunciation	Meaning
agonized (v)	ag' ə niz'd	suffered greatly over a decision; struggled
enamored (v)	en nam' êr'd	loved greatly; charmed with
loathed (v)	lōth'd	hated; detested
berserk (adv)	bêr sêrk'	crazy; out of control
devastated (v)	dev' ə stā təd	overwhelmed by sadness or disappointment
resented (v)	rē zen' təd	felt or expressed indignant displeasure
objectionable (adj)	əb jek' shən ə bel	causing disapproval
rebellious (adj)	rə bel' yəs	opposing authority
temperamental (adj)	tem prə men' təl	tending to unpredictable behavior
admonished (v)	ad mon' ish'd	warned or urged, gave earnest advice
earnestly (adv)	êr' nəst lē	seriously and sincerely
fallible (adj)	fal' ə bəl	capable of making a mistake

TRANSLATION

My parents struggled over whether to buy me a computer game which I loved, or a radio-controlled airplane, which I hated. My crazy, out-of-control behavior let them know I was terribly disappointed by their choice; and they let me know they were displeased by my authority-opposing, unpredictable behavior of which they strongly disapproved, and earnestly advised me to remember that everyone can make a mistake.

| SUPER SENTENCE 6 | Level One |

My uncle, an obese GOURMAND, with his usual APLOMB, approached the table at my cousin's wedding BANQUET with such ALACRITY (OBVIOUSLY lacking ADEQUATE FORESIGHT) that he INGESTED what he thought was a PALATABLE DELICACY, which was actually the table's centerpiece. How GAUCHE!

Word	Pronunciation	Meaning
obese (adj)	ō bēs'	very fat
gourmand (n)	gôr mä	person who appreciates fine food
aplomb (n)	ə plom'	complete confidence, assurance
banquet (n)	ban' kwet	dinner to honor someone
alacrity (adv)	ə lak' rə tē	cheerful readiness
obviously (adv)	ob' vē əs lē	clearly for all to see
adequate (adj)	ad' ə kwet	enough
foresight (n)	fôr' sīt	ability to see ahead
ingested (v)	in jes' təd	swallowed; ate
palatable (adj)	pal' ə tə bəl	pleasant tasting
delicacy (n)	del' i kə sē	something unusual to eat
gauche (adj)	gōsh	lacking in tact or the social graces; awkward

TRANSLATION

My very fat uncle, who appreciates fine food, with his usual complete confidence approached the table with such cheerful readiness at the dinner in honor of my cousin's wedding, (clearly lacking enough ability to see what was coming) that he ate what he thought was a pleasant tasting, rare treat, which was actually the table's centerpiece. How awkward!

SUPER SENTENCE 7	Level One

At the circus, a FOOLHARDY, LOQUACIOUS HAWKER stood in a GARGANTUAN, GARISHLY decorated wagon, trying to BAMBOOZLE and BEFUDDLE the people in the crowd, using LINGO to sell them a CONCOCTION which he ASSERTED would allow kids to PROCURE all A's in school if they IMBIBED one teaspoonful every morning.

Word	*Pronunciation*	*Meaning*
foolhardy (adj)	fül' hârd ē	foolishly adventurous
loquacious (adj)	lō kwā shəs	very talkative
hawker (n)	hä' kêr	one who talks a lot to sell something
gargantuan (adj)	gâr gan' choo	huge, gigantic
garishly (adv)	wən gār' ish lē	marred by loud colors or excessive ornamentation
bamboozle (v)	bam boo' zəl	to deceive by trickery
befuddle (v)	bē fud' əl	to confuse or dull one's senses
lingo (n)	lin' gō	language or words peculiar to a certain group, jargon
concoction (n)	kən kok' shən	strange mixture
asserted (v)	ə sîr təd	claimed, stated
procure (v)	prō kyûr'	obtain, get
imbibed (v)	im bib' d	drank

TRANSLATION

At the circus, a foolishly adventurous, talkative person who tries to sell things stood in a huge, tastelessly colorful wagon and tried to deceive with his tricks and confuse the senses of the people in the crowd, using peculiar words to sell them a strange mixture that he claimed would allow kids to earn all A's in school if they drank one teaspoonful every morning.

SUPER SENTENCE 8	Level One

Because she had DETECTED CHRONIC DEFICIENCIES in our spelling recently, our teacher declared an ULTIMATUM: either we RECTIFY the DECLINE in our scores and ACCRUE several CONSECUTIVE TRIUMPHS, or we would have to FORFEIT our place as the FOREMOST CONTRIBUTORS to the school newspaper.

Word	Pronunciation	Meaning
detected (v)	di tek' təd	discovered the existence of
chronic (adj)	krän' ik	habitual, repeated, recurring over a long period
deficiencies (n)	də fish' ən sēz	lack of acceptable standard
ultimatum (n)	ul ti mā' təm	final demand
rectify (v)	rek' ti fī	set something right
decline (v)	di klīn '	deteriorate gradually
accrue (v)	ə kroo '	accumulate
consecutive (adj)	kən sek' yə tiv	uninterrupted; one after another
triumphs (n)	trī ' umfs	victories
forfeit (v)	fôr' fit	lose the right to something
foremost (adj)	fôr' mōst	first in place or rank
contributors (n)	kən tri' byoo tərz	those who give something

TRANSLATION

Because she had discovered recurring, unacceptable performances in our spelling recently, our teacher announced a final demand: either we improve our deteriorating scores and collect several uninterrupted victories, or we would have to give up our place as the primary donators of articles to the school newspaper.

SUPER SENTENCE 9 | **Level One**

At the FESTIVE, TESTIMONIAL REPAST for our FLAMBOYANT, DAPPER, DEBONAIR principal, the guests ate RAVENOUSLY all the DELECTABLE TIDBITS which had been PAINSTAKINGLY prepared by our P.T.A.'s ENTERPRISING experts in the CULINARY arts.

Word	Pronunciation	Meaning
festive (adj)	fes' tiv	joyous, party-like
testimonial (adj)	tes tə mō' nē əl	expression of appreciation
repast (n)	rē' past	dinner, meal
flamboyant (adj)	flam boy' ənt	flashy, showy
dapper (adj)	dap' pêr	neat and trim in the way one dresses
debonair (adj)	deb ə nār'	gracefully charming
ravenously (adv)	rav' ən əs lē	very hungrily
delectable (adj)	də lek' tə bəl	enjoyable, delightful
tidbits (n)	tid' bits	choice bits of food
painstakingly (adv)	pān' stā king lē	with great care
enterprising (adj)	en' têr prī zing	bold; loving to experiment; adventuous; original
culinary (adj)	koo lin ār ē	related to the art of cooking

TRANSLATION

At the party-like meal to show appreciation for our flashy, neat and charming principal, the guests ate very hungrily all the enjoyable choice bits of food which had been carefully prepared by our P.T.A.'s adventurous experts in the cooking arts.

SUPER SENTENCE 10 | **Level One**

Tigers can be SAVAGE, FEROCIOUS, COMBATIVE animals. Tiger trainers should not be too ARROGANT or CONCEITED, or they might have to GRAPPLE DEFENSIVELY with a VORACIOUS, BELLIGERENT CARNIVORE that would APPARENTLY be VICTORIOUS.

Word	Pronunciation	Meaning
savage (adj)	sav' əj	wild, fierce
ferocious (adj)	fə rō' shus	fierce, savage
combative (adj)	kəm bat' iv	eager to fight
arrogant (adj)	ār' ə gənt	overconfident, having a feeling of superiority
conceited (adj)	kən sē' təd	having too high an opinion of oneself
grapple (v)	gra'pəl	seize or hold onto a struggling object
defensively (adv)	də fen' siv lē	intended to protect or defend
voracious (adj)	vō rā' shus	extremely hungry; ravenous
belligerent (adj)	bə lij' ər ənt	eager to fight
carnivore (n)	kâr' nə vôr	animal that eats other animals or humans
apparently (adj)	ə par' ənt lē	obviously; plainly; likely
victorious (adj)	vik tôr' ē əs	triumphant; winning

TRANSLATION

Tigers can be wild, fierce animals that are eager to fight. Tiger trainers should not be too over-confident or think too highly of their ability or they might have to try to grab, in order to defend themselves, an extremely hungry, ready-to-fight, flesh-eater that would likely be the winner.

SUPER SENTENCE 11 | **Level One**

For a career in AERONAUTICS, PREREQUISITES include a DAUNTLESS, HEROIC spirit, no QUEASINESS or ACROPHOBIA, the ability to SKILLFULLY operate TECHNICAL APPARATUS, and an ENERGETIC DEVOTION to the GLORY of American dominance in space.

Word	*Pronunciation*	*Meaning*
aeronautics (n)	ār ə no' tiks	the science of designing or flying aircraft
prerequisites (n)	prē rek' wi zits	things required beforehand
dauntless (adj)	dont' les	bravely determined
queasiness (n)	kwē' zē nəs	uneasy, somewhat sick feeling
acrophobia (n)	ak rə fō' bē ə	fear of heights
skillfully (adv)	skil' fəl lē	having well-trained ability
technical (adj)	tek' ni kəl	information connected to a science
apparatus (n)	ap ə rat' əs	equipment for a certain use or job
energetic (adj)	en êr jet' ik	having a lot of energy
devotion (n)	dē vō' shen	strong attachment to a person or job
glory (n)	glôr' ē	honor or praise
dominance (adj)	dom' ən əns	overcoming all others

TRANSLATION

For a career in flying aircraft, the things required beforehand include a bravely determined, courageous spirit, no uneasy feelings or fear of heights, the well-trained ability to operate equipment related to this science, and a strong attachment, accompanied by lots of energy, to the honor of the American ability to overcome all other countries in space.

LEVEL TWO ANSWERS

The CAITIFF USURPER, ACCOUTERED for MARAUDING with his JUNTA, sought IMPERIUM for the MOBOCRACY, unaware of the ANIMUS of the IMPUISSANT, LUMPEN DEMURRERS ready to IMMOLATE themselves for the sake of their causes.

Word	Pronunciation	Meaning
caitiff (adj)	kā' tif	mean, evil, dispicable, wretched
usurper (n)	yoo sûrp' êr	person who seizes power illegally
accoutered (v)	ə koo' têr'd	equipped, furnished
marauding (n)	mä rä' ding	roaming and looting
junta (n)	hoon' tə	military or political council
imperium (n)	im pir' ē əm	absolute power
mobocracy (n)	mo bo' krə sē	government by mob rule
animus (n)	an' i mus	hostility
impuissant (adj)	im pyoo' sənt	powerless
lumpen (adj)	loom' pən	of inferior status in their social class, degraded
demurrers (n)	də myûr' êrz	those who object
immolate (v)	im' mə lāt	sacrifice, usually in the interest of some cause

TRANSLATION

The evil power seizer, equipped for roaming and looting with his military council, tried to get absolute power for his government that was ruled by a mob, unaware of the hostility of the powerless, who objected to his plan and were ready to sacrifice themselves for their cause.

SUPER SENTENCE 2 | **Level Two**

The PRODIGIOUS and PROLIFIC COGNOSCENTE of modern music, FESTINATING to TRANSCRIBE the SCHERZO for winds and TIMPANI, TRUNCATED it to make a SEGUE between the ITERATIVE, ANTIPHONAL, and ISACOUSTIC sections of his new composition.

Word	Pronunciation	Meaning
prodigious (adj)	prə dij' əs	wonderful, amazing
prolific (adj)	prə lif' ik	abundant and often rapid productivity
cognoscente (n)	kon yō shen' tē	well-informed person
festinating (v)	fes' tin āt ing	hastening, hurrying
transcribe (v)	trans skrīb'	rewrite; arrange a musical composition for different instruments, often with modification or embellishment
scherzo (n)	skãr' tzō	playful musical composition in quick triple time
timpani (n)	tim' pən ē	a set of two or three kettle drums
truncated (v)	trun' kā təd	cut off a part; abbreviated
segue (n)	sā' gwā	transitional piece between musical numbers
iterative (adj)	it êr â' tiv	repetitious
antiphonal (adj)	an ti' fən əl	answering or alternating (voices or instruments)
isacoustic (adj)	ī sə kōo' stik	equally intense in sound

TRANSLATION

The extraordinary person, well-informed and abundantly productive in the art of modern music, hurrying to arrange the fast, playful piece for winds and kettle drums, shortened it to make a transitional piece between the equally intense in sound sections of his new composition that repetitiously alternated instruments.

SUPER SENTENCE 3	Level Two

The BRAGGADOCIO of the POETASTER is apparent as he writes his CLOYING DITHYRAMBS for ACCOLADES alone; while the ORGULOUS IAMBOGRAPHER has the METTLE and PANACHE to EXCOGITATE his LAMPOONS without GASCONADE.

Word	Pronunciation	Meaning
braggadocio (n)	brag ə dō' shē ō	empty boasting; arrogant pretension
poetaster (n)	pō' ət as têr	writer of poor poetry
cloying (adj)	kloy' ing	having an excess of sentimentality to the point of distaste
dithyrambs (n)	dith' ə ramz	choric poems of empassioned praise
accolades (n)	ak' ə lādz	recognition; bestowal of praise
orgulous (adj)	ôr' gyə ləs	proud
iambographer (n)	ī am bä' grə fêr	one noted for writing iambic lampoons
mettle (n)	met' təl	courage
panache (n)	pə näsh'	flair, elegant style, heroic flourish of manner
excogitate (v)	eks koj' i tāt	devise, contrive, think up; examine mentally in great detail
lampoons (n)	lam poonz '	aggressively controversial satire
gasconade (n)	gas' kən ād	excessive bragging

TRANSLATION

The arrogant pretension of the bad writer of poetry is apparent as he writes his distastefully sentimental choral poems of praise just for recognition; while the writer of iambic satire has the courage and heroic style to devise his controversial satires without excessive bragging.

SUPER SENTENCE 4   **Level Two**

The SENESCENT MYSTAGOGUE, DIVAGATING from LUCULENT interpretations and SPOUTING ABSTRUSE CANT, MESMERIZED the PURBLIND NEOPHYTES who were AGOG at his supposed SAGACITY.

Word	*Pronunciation*	*Meaning*
senescent (adj)	sə nes' ənt	aging
mystagogue (n)	mis' tə gog	interpreter of mysteries; teacher of mystical doctrines
divagating (v)	di və gā' ting	wandering, straying
luculent (adj)	lōo' kyōo lənt	clear; convincing
spouting (v)	spow' ting	pouring out words
abstruse (adj)	ab strōos '	hard to understand; hidden (idea)
cant (n)	kant	insincere talk; use of pious phraseology
mesmerized (v)	mez' mêr iz'd	caused to be spellbound; fascinated
purblind (adj)	pêr' blind	newly blind; comprehending imperfectly
neophyte (n)	nē' ō fit	new convert
agog (v)	ə gog'	eager; curious; excited; intensely interested
sagacity (n)	sə gas' ə tē	quality of being discerning; keenly perceptive

TRANSLATION

The aging teacher of mystical doctrines, straying from clear interpretations and pouring out hard-to-understand, pious phraseology, held spellbound the new converts who comprehended imperfectly and were excited about his supposed keen perception.

SUPER SENTENCE 5	Level Two

On a CHIVY with our FOWLING PIECES, we approached the CISMONTANE as an UNFORTUITOUS LEVANTER blew down. Encountering a SCREE, a CHAMOIS, and the EFFLUVIUMS of TRAVERTINES, we HOVE our rope, HEEZED ourselves up, and listened to a strange DIAPASON.

Word	Pronunciation	Meaning
chivy (n)	shiv' ē	chase or hunt
fowling pieces (adj)	fow' ling pēs əz	light gun for shooting birds or small animals
cismontane (n)	sis mon' tān	nearer side of a mountain
unfortuitous (adj)	un fôr too' ə tus	unlucky
levanter (n)	lə van' têr	strong, easterly Mediterranean wind
scree (n)	skrē	loose rock on a mountain slope, talus
chamois (n)	sham' ē or sham' wä	mountain antelope
effluviums (n)	e floo' vē ums	slight vapors; emanation; exhaust
travertines (n)	trav' êr tenz	mineral deposits around hot springs
hove (v)	hōv	threw; hurled; lifted
heezed (n)	hēz'd	hoisted; raised; pulled up
diapason (n)	di ə pā' zən	burst of (harmonious) sound

TRANSLATION

On a bird hunting chase with light guns, we approached the near side of the mountain as an unlucky strong easterly Mediterranean wind blew down. Encountering a slope of loose rock, a mountain antelope, and the slight vapors of hot springs mineral deposits, we hurled our rope, hoisted ourselves up, and listened to a burst of harmonious sound.

SUPER SENTENCE 6 | **Level Two**

The visiting PRELATE, INDAGATING MULTIFARIOUS aspects of TRADITIONALISM by virtue of his ACUMEN, labored in the CHANCEL by the SACRISTY door, resisting the impulse to SQUIB a POLEMICAL PAEAN which would have been a CONTRETEMPS to his colleagues in the CALEFACTORY.

Word	*Pronunciation*	*Meaning*
prelate (n)	pre' lət	high-ranking church official
indagating (n)	in' də gā ting	investigating; researching
multifarious (adj)	mult ə fa' rē əs	having great diversity or variety
traditionalism (n)	trə di' shun əl ism	doctrine or practices of those who follow tradition; orientation toward old established values
acumen (n)	ə kyoo' mən	superior mental ability
chancel (n)	chan' (t)sel	church area which contains altar, pulpit and lectern
sacristy (n)	sak' ris tē	room where sacred utensils and vestments are kept
squib (v)	skwib	write a witty, satirical attack
polemical (adj)	pə lem' i kəl	aggressively controversial; caustic
paean (n)	pē' ən	joyously exultant hymn
contretemps (n)	kon' trə tän	embarrassing occurrence
calefactory (n)	kal ə fak' tə rē	heated parlor in a monastery

TRANSLATION

The visiting high-ranking church official, researching the diverse aspects of the practice of established traditions easily because of his superior mental ability, worked in the pulpit area of the church by the door of the room where vestments are kept, resisting the impulse to write a witty satirical, caustic hymn which would have been an embarrassing occurrence to his colleagues in the heated parlor of the monastery.

SUPER SENTENCE 7   **Level Two**

The MEED for the PROFLIGATE GORMANDIZER, whose IRREFRAGABLY CORPULENT PHYSIOGNOMY betrayed his UNABSTEMIOUS HYPOSTASIS, and who refused to hold in ABEYANCE his DRACONIC appetite, was DYSPEPSIA and KATZENJAMMER.

Word	*Pronunciation*	*Meaning*
meed (n)	mēd	wage or reward; fitting return
profligate (adj)	pro' flə gət	completely given up to dissapation and liscentiousness, abandoned to vice and corruption
gormandizer (v)	gôr' mən dīz êr	lover of food who eats greedily
irrefragably (adj)	ir rə frag' ə blē	impossible to deny or dispute
corpulent (adj)	kôr' pyoo lənt	fat; obese; large body
physiognomy (adj)	fiz ē on' ə mē	outward features that show the inner qualities of mind or character
unabstemious (adj)	un ab ste' mē əs	not temperate in eating and drinking
hypostasis (n)	hī pō stäs' is	substance or rational nature of an individual
abeyance (n)	ə bā' əns	temporary suspension
draconic (adj)	drə kon' ik	dragon-like
dyspepsia (n)	dis pep' sē ə	indigestion
katzenjammer (n)	kat' zen jam êr	hangover

TRANSLATION

The fitting reward for the licentious lover of food, whose undeniably obese features betrayed his intemperate nature, and who refused to hold in temporary suspension his dragon-like appetite, was indigestion and a hangover.

SUPER SENTENCE 8 | **Level Two**

The UNCONSCIONABLE MALFEASANTS of the KAKISTOCRACY had a PROCLIVITY to PRATE INDEFATIGABLY in their own ARGOT and would JUGULATE any TIMOROUS PROSELYTE who held an opinion MINACIOUS or PARLOUS to them.

Word	*Pronunciation*	*Meaning*
unconscionable (adj)	un kon' shun ə bəl	not fair or just; outrageous
malfeasants (n)	mal fēz' ənts	officials guilty of wrong-doing, especially in connection with the office
kakistocracy (n)	kak i stok' rə se	government by the worst people in the country
proclivity (n)	prō kliv' i tē	natural tendency
prate (v)	prāt	to talk excessively; babble
indefatigably (adv)	in də fat' ə gə bəl	continuing unremittingly, untiringly
argot (n)	är gō	special vocabulary that belongs to a particular group or profession; jargon
jugulate (v)	jōō' gyu lāt	cut the throat of
timorous (adj)	tim' êr əs	fearfu;, timid
proselyte (n)	pros' ə līt	a convert to a new belief
minacious (adj)	mi nā' shus	menacing; threatening
parlous (adj)	pâr' ləs	perilous; dangerous

TRANSLATION

The unjust public officers (guilty of wrongdoing) in the government run by the worst people in the country had a natural tendency to babble untiringly in their own jargon, and would cut the throat of any timid convert who held an opinion threatening or dangerous to them.

SUPER SENTENCE 9	Level Two

In CARTOMANCY, PRESTIDIGITATORS who use OBFUSCATION and PETTIFOGGERY may live in OBLOQUY if a CHARY, INDEFECTIBLE HARBINGER of justice arises whose ONUS is to expose the FEIGNED VERSIMILITUDE of the practitioners as CHICANERY.

Word	*Pronunciation*	*Meaning*
cartomancy (n)	kär' tə man sē	art of fortune-telling using playing cards
prestidigitators (n)	pres tə dij' ə tā têrz	magicians
obfuscation (n)	ob fus kā' shun	act of bewildering, confusing
pettifoggery (n)	ped' e fog ə rē	the practice of engaging in legal chicanery; quibbling over insignificant details
obloquy (n)	ob' lə kwē	disgrace; defaming utterances
chary (adj)	char' ē	careful; cautious
indefectible (adj)	in də fek' tə bəl	faultless; flawless; incorruptible
harbinger (n)	hâr' bin jêr	herald of what lies ahead
onus (n)	ō' nus	burde;, duty that involves considerable difficulty
feigned (adj)	fānd	not genuine; insincere
versimilitude (n)	vêr sə mil' ə tüd	something that appears to be truthful
chicanery (n)	shi kā' nə rē	trickery; deception

TRANSLATION

In the art of fortune telling by using cards, magicians who use confusion and legal trickery may live in disgrace if a cautious, incorruptible herald of justice arises whose difficult duty is to expose the pretended appearance of truth of the practitioners as deception.

SUPER SENTENCE 10   **Level Two**

The MEWLING, INCONTINENT NEONATES are PURPORTED to REEK VENIAL, NOISOME FETORS similar to those EMINATING from a NOXIOUS, MEPHITIC CARAVANSERAI.

Word	Pronunciation	Meaning
mewling (adj)	myool' ing	crying, whimpering
incontinent (adj)	in kon' tə nənt	unable to hold back one's bodily functions
neonates (n)	ne' ə nāts	newborn babies
purported (v)	pēr pôr' təd	claimed
reek (v)	rēk	give off a strong, offensive odor
venial (adj)	vē' nē əl	excusable; forgivable; minor
noisome (adj)	noy' səm	disgusting; offensive to the sense of smell
fetors (n)	fe' tərz	a strong, offensive odor; stench
eminating (v)	em' ən āt ing	emitting, giving out from a source
noxious (adj)	nok' shəs	harmful to one's health
mephitic (adj)	mə fit' ik	offensive to the smell
caravanserai (n)	kar ə van' sə ri	an inn with a large courtyard in which camels rest overnight

TRANSLATION

The crying babies with soiled diapers are claimed to give off excusable, disgusting odors similar to those surrounding an unhealthful, smelly inn where camels rest overnight.

SUPER SENTENCE 11   **Level Two**

The TRUCULENT, OPPIDAN LICKSPITTLE SEQUESTERED himself from the BROUHAHA caused by the PUSILLANIMOUS MOUNTEBANK, and MACHINATED a MACHIAVELLIAN PREVARICATION to METE to himself some of the mountebank's LUCRE.

Word	Pronunciation	Meaning
truculent (adj)	truk' yə lənt	fierce, cruel, belligerent, pugnacious
oppidan (adj)	op' i dən	townsperson
lickspittle (n)	lik' spit əl	a flatterer; a Toady
sequestered (v)	sə kwes' têr'd	secluded; separated
brouhaha (n)	broo hä' hä	excited clamor or confusion; hubbub
pusillanimous (adj)	pyoo sə lan' ə məs	cowardly
mountebank (n)	mown' tə bangk	a charlatan or quack; one who sells pills or fake potions
machinated (v)	mak' ə nāt əd	contrived or devised; plotted
machiavellian (adj)	mak ē ə vel' ē ən	resembling a political theory put forth by Machiavelli involving manipulation, duplicity; the belief that the end justifies the means
prevarication (n)	prē vār ə kā' shun	lie
mete (v)	mēt	distribute by careful measure, allot
lucre (n)	loo' kər	monetary collection; profit

TRANSLATION

The cruel flatterer from the town separated himself from the confusion caused by the cowardly charlatan, and devised a cleverly manipulative lie to allot to himself some of the mountebank's profit.